Opal Huber
Oct 2 - 70

D0021198

Avanelle Day's
HERB & SPICE SAMPLER COOKBOOK

ILLUSTRATIONS BY ROB COBUZIO
GRAMERCY PUBLISHING COMPANY • NEW YORK

Avanelle Day is the co-author with Lillie Stuckey of *The Spice Cookbook,* the *complete* book of spice and herb cookery which contains 1400 superb recipes for American and international cuisine. Mrs. Day received her Master's Degree in home economics from Columbia College and has tested and perfected thousands of recipes, using all known varieties of spices.

Library of Congress catalog card number:
67–25923
This edition published by Gramercy Publishing Company, a division of Crown Publishers, Inc., by arrangement with David White Company
d e f g h
Printed in the United States of America

CONTENTS

CONTENTS

INTRODUCTION

The recent increased popularity of herbs and spices is probably the greatest thing that has happened to American cookery since the Indians introduced the Pilgrims to corn. No dish, however routine, will ever be dull when these subtle flavorings are skillfully and discreetly added. Their number and variety are astonishing; their uses range throughout the entire menu. Most of them have been known and used since history began. To the romantic-minded their very names can be exciting: cinnamon and mace conjure up the scented breezes that told sailors they were near the Spice Islands; rosemary, chervil, and thyme recall the loaenge-shaped herb gardens of medieval monks.

Today the most exotic spices as well as the homelier herbs are available in every supermarket. Also, if you are so minded, many herbs can easily be grown in the garden, or even on a windowsill, affording the pleasure of having the fresh leaves. The cook's only problem is to learn their uses and this book will help her there.

WHAT ARE HERBS AND SPICES?

In the broad sense the word "spice" is used to designate any aromatic product of vegetable origin which adds zest to food. Separating these seasonings into categories is difficult, since the usual division into "herbs" and "spices" involves many borderline cases. The following classification may help to clarify the situation:

True spices: seeds, fruits, barks, or roots of various plants native to the tropics; examples are allspice, cinnamon, cloves, ginger, mace, nutmeg, pepper. Spices are always dried; some are available whole as well as powdered.

Herbs: plants grown in the temperate zones, the leaves of which are used fresh or dried; among these are basil, chervil, marjoram, oregano, rosemary, savory, sage, thyme.

Aromatic seeds: seeds of various herbs, some grown in hot climates, some in mild, some in either. These include anise, caraway, coriander, cumin, dill, and poppy seeds. The seeds are classed as spices, but in some cases the leaves are also used as herbs.

The lists on the endpapers include the spices and herbs most frequently used in cooking and suggestions for foods to which each is well adapted.

HOW TO USE THEM IN COOKING

The judicious use of spices (in the broad sense of the term) is a fundamental secret of good cooking. These "mighty mites" add flavor, aroma, and in some cases color; and the savory smell of the cooking food will stimulate appetites before the meal is even served. If you have been wanting to cook with spices but have been afraid to experiment, here are a few important rules to guide you.

1. Start by adding a few familiar spices to some of your family dishes to find out for yourself how they improve the flavor. Then try some of the less familiar spices to increase your knowledge.

2. Use spices with a light hand—the aromatic oils are strong, and too much of any flavor is objectionable. Always keep in mind that spices should enhance the flavor of a dish, not disguise it.

3. Since each spice, herb, or seed has a different degree of pungency, no blanket rule as to amount can be given. When trying something new, follow a reliable recipe. Later you can vary the seasoning to suit the taste of your family. The seasoning should be so subtle that only the expert will be able to identify the spice that was added. An exception to this rule is a dish which features one particular flavor, such as chili con carne, curries, or gingerbread. In case no recipe is available it is safe to begin with ¼ teaspoon of spice or herb

(less for hot or strong-flavored ones, such as pepper or garlic) in a 6-portion recipe. This quantity may be increased after testing.

4. Learn the art of blending spices and herbs. A good rule is to combine one spice or herb that has a strong flavor with one, two, or three others that have less pronounced flavor. Example: rosemary with thyme and parsley.

5. Generally speaking, ground spices, herbs, and seeds should be added to dishes shortly before the cooking is completed, since long cooking destroys their flavor and aroma. Whole spices should be added to long-cooking dishes—soups, stews, ragouts, pot roast—at the beginning of the cooking period. In dishes which are not cooked, salads, and salad dressings, the spices should be added well before serving time.

6. Keep in mind that the flavor of dried herbs is three to four times stronger than that of fresh herbs, therefore three or four times as much of the latter may be used.

HOW TO STORE THEM

Spices, herbs, and seeds contain essential aromatic oils, which give them their characteristic flavor and color.

These oils evaporate with keeping and the products lose their flavor and strength. Therefore, it is wise to buy them in small packages and replace them often. Sniff the jars frequently to see if the delicate aroma is still there. If it has faded, you need to replace the spice. Keep jars or cans tightly closed. Spices purchased in cardboard boxes should be transferred to jars and the jars tightly closed. Store in a clean, cool, dry place away from sunlight and any source of heat; do not be tempted by convenience to keep spices near the kitchen stove.

Avanelle Day

APPETIZERS

Avocado Dip

1 medium-sized ripe avocado

4 teaspoons fresh lemon juice

2 tablespoons mayonnaise

¾ teaspoon salt or salt to taste

2 teaspoons grated onion

1/16 teaspoon garlic juice

4 drops Red Hot Sauce

3 tablespoons finely chopped fresh tomatoes

chopped parsley

Peel the avocado and cut it into small dice. Add the lemon juice. Mash the avocado until smooth, or purée it in an electric blender. Add all the remaining ingredients except the parsley. Mix well. Place the dip in a small serving bowl and sprinkle with chopped parsley. Serve as a dip for vegetable sticks, potato chips, or unsweetened crackers. Makes 1 scant cup.

Caraway-Seed–Cream-Cheese Dip

1 teaspoon powdered mustard	¼ cup (½ stick) unsalted butter
2 teaspoons water	1 ¼ teaspoons salt
8-ounce package cream cheese	2 tablespoons paprika
	4 teaspoons caraway seed

Blend the mustard with the water and let stand 5 minutes to develop the flavor. Add all the remaining ingredients and mix until the mixture is fluffy. Chill. Remove from the refrigerator about 1 hour before serving. Serve as a dip for vegetable sticks, potato chips, or unsweetened crackers. Makes 1 ¼ cups.

Chopped Chicken Livers and Hard-Cooked Eggs

½ cup finely chopped onion	⅛ teaspoon ground black pepper
6 tablespoons chicken fat or butter	⅛ teaspoon instant garlic
1 pound chicken livers	rye bread, rye crackers, or other crackers
2 hard-cooked eggs	chopped parsley
1 ¼ teaspoons salt	1 hard-cooked egg yolk

Cook the onion in 2 tablespoons of the chicken fat or butter 3 to 4 minutes or until soft. Trim the membranes from the livers and cut each liver in half. Put the livers on a rack in the broiler pan and place it in the broiler 4 inches from the source of heat. Broil the livers 6 minutes on one side, turn, and broil 1 minute longer. Put the livers and the eggs through a food chopper, using the fine blade, or put them in an electric blender and blend them almost to a purée. Add the cooked onion, the remaining 4 tablespoons chicken fat or butter, and the salt, black pepper, and garlic. Mix well. Serve on rounds or squares of rye bread, rye crackers, or other crackers. Garnish with chopped parsley and bits of hard-cooked egg yolk. Makes 2 cups.

Ham Canapés

About 2 dozen 2-inch rounds or squares of firm-textured bread

4 to 5 tablespoons butter or margarine

2 tablespoons finely chopped onion

1 cup ground cooked ham

dash ground black pepper

¼ cup sour cream

¼ teaspoon powdered mustard

½ teaspoon water

chopped parsley

Fry one side of each round or square of bread in the butter or margarine, adding it as needed, then toast the reverse side in the broiler oven, 4 inches from the source of heat. Set aside. Combine the next 4 ingredients. Blend the mustard with the water, let stand 5 minutes to develop the flavor, and then add to the ham mixture. Spread the mixture over the buttered side of the rounds or squares of bread. Decorate with chopped parsley. Makes approximately 2 dozen canapés.

Hot Cheese Canapés

¼ teaspoon powdered
  mustard
½ teaspoon water
1½ cups (6 ounces)
  grated Cheddar cheese
⅛ teaspoon ground black
  pepper

¼ teaspoon ground ginger
2 tablespoons dry sherry
9 slices firm-textured
  bread
5 to 6 tablespoons butter
  or margarine
chopped parsley

Blend the mustard with the water, let it stand 5 minutes, and then add to the cheese. Add the black pepper, ginger, and sherry. Mix until smooth. Trim the crusts from the bread slices, and cut each slice into 4 squares or triangles. Sauté the squares or triangles on one side in butter or margarine, adding it as needed, and toast the other side under the broiler heat. Spread the cheese mixture over the buttered side of the bread, covering the bread to the edges. Place under broiler heat 1 to 2 minutes, or until cheese has melted and is flecked with brown. Garnish with chopped parsely. Makes 3 dozen.

Sesame-Seed Cheese and Olive Balls

Use green stuffed olives. Roll each in cream cheese, then in toasted sesame seed. Refrigerate until ready to serve. Serve as an appetizer or use as a garnish for salads. Allow 3 balls per person for serving as an appetizer or 1 ball as a garnish on a salad plate.

Spiced Nuts

1 cup blanched almonds, whole pecan halves, or cashew nuts
2 tablespoons butter

1 teaspoon curry powder or chili powder
salt to taste

Fry the nuts in the butter in a heavy skillet over moderate heat, stirring constantly. Remove the skillet from the heat and turn the nuts out onto paper towels to drain. Sprinkle with chili powder or curry powder and with salt to taste. Makes 1 cup.

BEVERAGES

Hot or cold beverages, such as tea and punch, may be flavored with spices or herbs. If dried herbs are used, brew them in a small amount of liquid and then strain the liquid into fruit juices or tea. If fresh herbs, such as mint or rosemary, are used, just add the sprigs to the prepared juices. Whole spices need to be cooked with the sugar syrup.

Wassail, American Style

This is a non-alcoholic American version. The authentic English wassail, made of spiced ale or beer, wine, and baked apples, is served on festive occasions, such as Christmas and Twelfth Night, and traditionally served to carol singers.

3 cups apple cider
1 cup pineapple juice
1½ cups orange juice
½ cup grapefruit juice
½ cup lemon juice
¼ cup sugar
2 sticks cinnamon, each 2 inches long

1½ teaspoons whole allspice
½ teaspoon whole cloves

wine to taste (optional)
orange slices studded with whole cloves

Put the first 7 ingredients in a 2½-quart saucepan. Tie the allspice and cloves in a cheesecloth bag and add to the juices. Bring the mixture to boiling point, reduce heat, and simmer 5 minutes. To prevent the hot punch from cracking a glass punch bowl, put a silver punch ladle in the bowl, then pour in the hot juices. Discard the spice bag, but leave in the cinnamon sticks. (If desired, add wine to taste.) Float the clove-studded orange slices over the surface. Makes 1½ quarts or 12 servings.

Spiced Party Cocoa

½ cup sugar
½ cup cocoa
1 cup boiling water
⅛ teaspoon salt
12 whole cloves

4 cups milk
1 cup light cream
½ teaspoon vanilla extract
8 cinnamon sticks, each 4 to 6 inches long

Put the first 5 ingredients in a 2½-quart saucepan or in the top of a double boiler and mix well. Bring the mixture to boiling point, and stir and cook over moderate heat for 3 minutes. Add the milk, cream, and vanilla extract. Cook over low heat or hot water until the cocoa is hot, stirring frequently to prevent a skin from forming over the surface. Beat the cocoa with a rotary beater or a wire whisk 1 to 2 minutes or until bubbles form over the top. Serve hot in mugs with a long stick of cinnamon in each to use as a muddler. Makes 6 cups (8 servings).

BREADS

Blueberry Muffins

1¾ cups sifted all-purpose flour	2 large eggs, beaten
½ teaspoon salt	¾ cup milk
2½ teaspoons double-acting baking powder	1 teaspoon vanilla extract
¾ teaspoon ground mace	⅓ cup shortening, melted
¾ cup sugar	1 cup blueberries
	granulated sugar

Sift the first 5 ingredients together into a mixing bowl. Combine the eggs, milk, and vanilla extract and add the mixture to the dry ingredients. Add the shortening. Mix only until the ingredients are blended, using about 28 strokes. (If the batter is stirred too much, large tunnels will form in it.) Stir in the blueberries. Drop the batter into well-greased, lightly floured 2½-inch muffin cups, filling them about three-fourths full. Sprinkle ½ teaspoon sugar over each muffin. Bake in a preheated moderate oven (375° F.) 20 to 25 minutes, or until the muffins have browned. Serve hot. Makes 14 muffins.

Cheese Fan Biscuits

1 package ready-to-cook biscuits
¼ cup (½ stick) butter or margarine, melted

¾ teaspoon paprika
½ cup grated sharp Cheddar cheese

Arrange the biscuits on a board and cut each in half. Mix the melted buter or margarine with the paprika. Dip each half biscuit in the mixture, and then dredge in grated cheese. Lightly butter 2 cupcake pans, each containing 6 individual cups 2½ inches across the top. Stand 3 biscuit halves in each cup. Bake in a preheated hot oven (425° F.) 12 to 15 minutes, or until the biscuits have browned. Serve hot. Makes 12 biscuits.

CAKES AND COOKIES

Sweet spices are used generously in many recipes for cakes and cookies, and in others are added with a light hand to give the batter delicate flavor. Since fats are good mediums for absorbing spice flavor, cakes and cookies are more pleasing if the spices are blended with the butter or shortening instead of being sifted with the flour as most recipes specify.

Cakes

Brown-Sugar Pineapple Cake

1 teaspoon soda
¾ teaspoon ground nut-
  meg
¼ teaspoon salt
1 teaspoon vanilla extract

¾ cup (1½ sticks) but-
  ter or margarine

1 cup light brown sugar,
  firmly packed
2 large eggs

2 cups sifted all-purpose flour

1 cup (8¾-ounce can) crushed pineapple

¼ cup water

Caramel Frosting (see following recipe)

Put the first 5 ingredients in a mixing bowl and mix well. Gradually blend in the sugar. Beat in the eggs, one at a time. Add flour alternately with the pineapple and water, beginning and ending with flour. Turn the batter into 2 well-greased, lightly floured, round 8-inch cake pans. Bake in a preheated moderate oven (375° F.) 30 minutes or until a cake tester or toothpick inserted in the center comes out clean. Cool the layers in the pans 10 minutes, then turn them out onto wire racks to finish cooling. Spread the Caramel Frosting between the layers and over the top. Makes one 8-inch 2-layer cake.

CARAMEL FROSTING   Put in a 2-quart saucepan 2 cups light brown sugar, ½ cup milk, ½ cup (1 stick) butter or margarine, and a dash of salt. Mix well. Bring the mixture to boiling point, and boil 2 minutes by the clock. Remove from the heat and beat until the frosting is creamy. Let the frosting stand until it is cool, then beat again until it is firm enough to spread. Makes frosting for one 8-inch 2-layer cake.

Chocolate Pecan Upside-Down Cake

PECAN TOPPING

¼ cup light brown sugar
¼ teaspoon ground cinnamon
¼ cup (½ stick) softened butter or margarine
1 cup pecan halves
¾ cup light corn syrup

Gradually blend the sugar and cinnamon with the butter or margarine. Add the pecans and mix well. Blend in the corn syrup. Spread the mixture uniformly over the bottom of a 9- by 9- by 2-inch cake pan. Set aside.

CHOCOLATE CAKE BATTER

2 squares (2 ounces) unsweetened chocolate

½ teaspoon salt
½ teaspoon ground cinnamon
1½ teaspoons vanilla extract
6 tablespoons softened butter or margarine
1⅓ cups sugar
2 large eggs
2 cups sifted all-purpose flour
2 teaspoons double-acting baking powder
1¼ cups milk

Put the chocolate in a custard cup and set the cup in a pan of hot water over very low heat until chocolate is melted. Put the next 4 ingredients in a mixing bowl and stir until they are blended. Gradually add the sugar, mixing well after each addition. Stir in the melted chocolate. Beat in the eggs, one at a time. Sift the flour again with the baking powder and add gradually, alternately with the milk, beginning and ending with the flour. Beat the batter ½ minute. Pour the batter over the Pecan Topping in the cake pan. Bake in a preheated slow oven (325° F.) 1 hour. Remove the cake from the oven and let it stand in the pan for 15 minutes. Then loosen the cake from the sides of the pan with a spatula and turn it out onto a wire rack to finish cooling. Cut into squares to serve. Makes 9 to 12 servings.

Gingerbread

½ cup shortening
½ teaspoon salt
1½ teaspoons soda
½ teaspoon ground allspice
¾ teaspoon ground cinnamon

½ teaspoon ground cloves
1 teaspoon ground ginger
½ teaspoon ground nutmeg
___
1 cup sugar
1 large egg

1 cup sugar-cane syrup

2½ cups sifted all-purpose flour

1 cup hot water

whipped cream or Golden Lemon Sauce

Mix the shortening with the salt, soda, and spices. Gradually add the sugar, mixing well after each addition. Beat in the egg. Add the syrup alternately with the flour. Stir in the hot water, a little at a time, mixing well after each addition. Turn the batter into a well-greased, lightly floured 9- by 9- by 2-inch baking pan or a 13- by 9- by 2-inch baking pan. Bake in a preheated moderate oven (350° F.) 55 to 60 minutes, or until a toothpick inserted in the center comes out clean. Serve warm or cold, topped with whipped cream or Golden Lemon Sauce. Makes 9 to 12 servings.

Cookies

Butter-Pecan Balls

½ cup granulated sugar

½ teaspoon ground ginger

½ teaspoon ground mace

1 cup (2 sticks) butter or

margarine, softened

1 cup chopped pecans

2 cups sifted all-purpose flour

sifted confectioners' sugar

Gradually add the granulated sugar, ginger, and mace to the butter or margarine, mixing well after each addition. Stir in the pecans, and then the flour, ⅓ cup at a time. Chill the dough until it is stiff enough to handle, 2 to 3 hours. Shape into 1-inch balls and place them 1 inch apart on ungreased cooky sheets. Bake in a preheated slow oven (325° F.) 20 to 25 minutes or until cookies have begun to brown lightly at the bottom. The tops of the cookies should remain white. Transfer to a wire cooling rack, roll in sifted confectioners' sugar, cool, and roll again in confectioners' sugar. Store in an airtight container. Makes 4 dozen cookies.

Date-and-Nut Fudge Bars

⅔ cup sifted all-purpose flour
⅛ teaspoon soda
¼ teaspoon salt
¾ teaspoon ground cinnamon

⅓ cup shortening
2 squares unsweetened chocolate

1 cup light brown sugar
2 teaspoons vanilla extract
2 large eggs
2 tablespoons milk
½ cup chopped nuts
¼ cup finely chopped dried dates
pecan halves (decoration)

Sift together the first 4 ingredients and set aside. In the top part of a double boiler, large enough for mixing the cookies, melt the shortening and chocolate over hot water. Add the sugar and vanilla and mix well. Beat in the eggs. Stir in the milk and the flour mixture. Blend in the nuts and dates. Turn the batter into a well-greased, lightly floured 9- by 9- by 2-inch baking pan, and spread it uniformly over the bottom. Bake in a preheated moderate oven (350° F.) 45 minutes or until toothpick inserted in the center comes out clean. Turn the cake out onto a wire rack. While it is still warm, cut into 32 bars, and lightly press a pecan half in the center of each. Store in an airtight container. Makes 32 bars.

RAISIN-AND-NUT-FUDGE BARS Replace the dates in the preceding recipe with ¼ cup seedless raisins.

Fruit-and-Nut Cooky Bars

This delicious bar cooky is my favorite.

1 cup (2 sticks) butter or margarine	½ teaspoon soda
	½ teaspoon salt
1 teaspoon double-acting baking powder	1 teaspoon ground cinnamon

¾ teaspoon ground nutmeg

½ teaspoon ground cloves

1½ cups sugar

3 large eggs

1¼ cups dried and candied fruits (dates, raisins or currants, and mixed candied fruits)

¾ cup chopped pecans or walnuts

4 cups sifted all-purpose flour

Caramel Icing (see following recipe)

Have all ingredients at room temperature. Put the first 7 ingredients into a large mixing bowl and mix them well. Gradually blend in 1 cup of the sugar. Beat in 1 of the eggs and then blend in the remaining ½ cup sugar. Beat in the remaining 2 eggs. Stir in the fruits and nuts. Add the flour, a little at a time, mixing after each addition. Chill the dough 1 hour or until it is stiff enough to handle. With the hands, roll the dough, on a lightly floured surface, into rolls 1 inch in diameter and the length of the cooky sheet. (This amount of dough is enough for 9 rolls.) Put 2 rolls, lengthwise, on a greased cooky sheet, 3 inches apart to allow room for spreading. With the fingers flatten the rolls to ¼ inch thickness, keeping the edges straight. Bake them in a preheated moderate oven (350° F.) 12 to 15 minutes, Remove from the oven and while the strips are still

warm, cut them crosswise into bars 1½ inches wide.
Then quickly brush the tops with Caramel Icing, using
a pastry brush or an artists' small narrow paint brush
reserved for use as a pastry brush. Cool the bars on
wire racks. Repeat until all the rolls are baked. Store
them in airtight containers. Makes 6½ dozen bars.

CARAMEL ICING

1 cup light brown sugar	½ cup hot water
¼ cup (½ stick) butter or margarine	½ teaspoon vanilla extract

Put the first 3 ingredients in a 1-quart saucepan, place
the saucepan over moderate heat, and stir the mixture
until the sugar has dissolved and the butter has melted.
Continue cooking, without stirring, to 236° F. on a
candy thermometer, or until a soft ball forms when a
little (about ¼ teaspoonful) of the syrup is dropped in
cold water. Remove the syrup from the heat, add the
vanilla extract, and beat about 1½ minutes or until the
syrup begins to cloud. While the syrup is still in a
liquid state, brush it over the tops of the cooky bars. To
keep the syrup liquid while the cookies finish baking,
stand the saucepan in another pan of hot water. Makes
enough icing for 6½ dozen bars.

Nutmeg Butter Wafers

2 cups sifted all-purpose flour

2 teaspoons double-acting baking powder

½ teaspoon salt

1 cup sugar

¾ teaspoon ground nutmeg

1½ teaspoons vanilla extract

⅔ cup softened butter or margarine

1 large egg

1 cup milk

Sift the flour with the baking powder and salt and reserve. Gradually blend the sugar with the nutmeg, vanilla extract, and butter or margarine. Beat in the egg. Gradually add the flour mixture alternately with the milk. Drop rounded ½ teaspoonfuls of the dough onto ungreased cooky sheets, 1½ inches apart to allow room for spreading. Flatten the cookies to ¹⁄₁₆ inch thickness with a glass covered with a wet cloth. Bake in a preheated moderate oven (350° F.) 10 to 12 minutes or until the cookies have browned lightly around the edges. Transfer to a wire cooling rack to cool. Store in airtight containers. Makes 4½ dozen 2-inch cookies.

Rolled Christmas Cookies

4 cups sifted all-purpose flour

1½ cups sugar

½ teaspoon salt

1 teaspoon ground ginger

1 teaspoon ground allspice

1½ cups (3 sticks) butter or margarine

2 large eggs, lightly beaten

2 tablespoons cold water

Confectioners' Sugar and Water Icing (see following recipe)

candied fruit, colored candy decorettes, cinnamon drops, silver dragées, or seeded raisins

Sift the first 5 ingredients together into a mixing bowl. Add the butter or margarine and cut it in to form a mixture that resembles coarse meal. Stir in the eggs and the water, mixing well. (This dough will be stiff, but do not add more water.) Chill the dough 1 hour or until it is stiff enough to handle easily. Roll out onto a lightly floured surface to ⅛-inch thickness. Use assorted cooky cutters, dipped in flour, to cut the cookies. Bake them on an ungreased cooky sheet in a preheated hot oven (400° F.) 7 to 8 minutes or until they have browned lightly around the edges. Transfer cookies to wire racks to cool. Frost as desired with Confectioners' Sugar and Water Icing. Decorate as desired with candied fruit, colored candy decorettes, cinnamon drops, silver dragées, or seeded raisins. Or, if desired, decorate the cookies with candied fruit before they are baked. Store in airtight containers. Makes approximately 9 dozen cookies.

CONFECTIONERS' SUGAR AND WATER ICING   Mix 4 teaspoons water with 1 cup sifted confectioners' sugar until the mixture is smooth and can be spread easily. Tint the icing as desired with vegetable food coloring, starting with 2 drops and adding more until the desired color is reached. The icing may be put on the cookies with a cake decorators' tube, spread with a spatula, or painted on with an artists' small paint brush saved for that purpose. Make additional icing as needed. Makes approximately 1/3 cup.

CHEESE AND EGG DISHES

Cheese and eggs blend harmoniously with most of the herbs and nonsweet spices.

Puffy Cheese Pudding

¼ teaspoon powdered mustard

1 teaspoon water

2 cups soft breadcrumbs

1¾ cups milk

1¾ cups (½ pound) grated Cheddar cheese

¾ teaspoon salt

¼ teaspoon ground ginger

dash cayenne

1 tablespoon butter or margarine, melted

1 large whole egg

3 large eggs, separated

Mix the mustard with the water and let stand 5 minutes to develop the flavor. Soak the breadcrumbs in the milk until they have absorbed all the milk. Add the mustard and the next 5 ingredients. Beat the whole egg and the 3 egg yolks together and blend with the cheese mixture. Beat the egg whites until they stand in soft stiff peaks when the beater is slowly raised, being careful not to beat them too dry, and gently fold them into the mixture. Turn the mixture into an ungreased 1-quart casserole. Place it in a pan of hot water and bake in a preheated slow oven (325° F.) 1¼ hours. Serve promptly. Makes 6 servings.

Quiche Lorraine

(Main-Dish Cheese Pie)

½ teaspoon powdered mustard
1 teaspoon water
1 unbaked 9-inch 1-crust pie shell
6 strips crisply fried bacon, cut in half
12 thin slices Swiss cheese or Gruyère cheese

4 large eggs
1 tablespoon flour
½ teaspoon salt
dash cayenne
2 cups light cream
1½ teaspoons butter or margarine, melted

Blend the mustard with the water and let the mixture stand 5 minutes. Line the unbaked pastry shell with the bacon and cheese slices. Beat the eggs with the mustard, flour, salt, and cayenne. Add the cream and the melted butter or margarine and strain the mixture over the bacon and cheese. Bake in a preheated moderate oven (375° F.) 40 minutes or until the custard is set. Makes one 9-inch pie (6 servings).

Scrambled Eggs, Texas Style

1 tablespoon bacon drippings
¼ cup finely chopped onion
¼ cup finely chopped green pepper
___
8 large eggs, lightly beaten
6 tablespoons light cream or milk

½ teaspoon salt
¼ teaspoon ground black pepper
⅟₁₆ teaspoon garlic powder (optional)
1 teaspoon chili powder
6 slices crisp bacon, crumbled
___
¼ cup (½ stick) butter or margarine, melted

Heat the bacon drippings in a 9-inch heavy skillet. Add the onion and green pepper, and cook until they are soft, 4 to 5 minutes. Combine the next 7 ingredients, add to the onion and green pepper, and stir and cook over low heat until the eggs are set, 6 to 7 minutes. Spoon a little melted butter over each serving. Makes 6 servings. For lunch or supper serve with hashed brown potatoes, sliced tomatoes, Cheese Fan Biscuits, butter, and grapefruit or melon.

Scrambled Salmon and Eggs

3 tablespoons butter or margarine
1-pound can pink or red salmon, undrained
4 large eggs
1 tablespoon fine dry breadcrumbs

2 teaspoons cider vinegar
¼ teaspoon dried thyme
¾ teaspoon salt
⅛ teaspoon ground black pepper
chopped parsley

Melt the butter or margarine in a 9- or 10-inch skillet. Flake the salmon but do not drain. Add it to the butter or margarine. Stir in all the remaining ingredients, except the parsley. Cook over moderately low heat, stirring constantly, 6 to 7 minutes or until the mixture is hot and the eggs have set. Sprinkle with chopped parsley. Makes 6 servings.

CHILI DISHES

Chili powder, a blend usually made of Mexican chili pepper, oregano, cumin, and garlic salt, is the basic seasoning in many southwestern dishes in addition to chili con carne. It is also used with shellfish, stews, scrambled eggs, and meats.

Barbecued Meat and Cheese Patties, Western Style

1½ pounds ground chuck
6 thin slices American cheese
salt and ground black pepper
___
3 tablespoons shortening

⅓ cup finely chopped green pepper
½ cup finely chopped onion
___
¾ cup Spanish-style tomato sauce

1½ tablespoons cider vinegar

1½ teaspoons chili powder, or chili powder to taste

½ teaspoon garlic powder, or 1 small clove garlic, split

½ cup coffee, or ¾ teaspoon instant coffee and ½ cup water

_____

6 warmed hamburger buns, or 3 cups hot cooked rice

Shape the chuck into 12 patties ¼ inch thick. Cut the cheese slices to fit the patties and place one on each of 6 patties. Cover with the remaining 6 patties, and pinch the edges together firmly so that the cheese does not show. Sprinkle both sides of the patties with salt and black pepper. Heat 2 tablespoons of the shortening in a heavy 10-inch skillet, add the patties, and brown them on both sides. Remove the patties from the skillet and keep them warm. Put the remaining 1 tablespoon shortening in the skillet, add the green pepper and onion, and cook them until they are soft, 4 to 5 minutes. Add the next 5 ingredients and bring to boiling point. Reduce heat, add patties, cover, and cook 10 minutes or until the sauce has thickened. (If a garlic clove was used, remove and discard.) Adjust the salt and black pepper. Serve the patties in warmed hamburger buns

with a little of the sauce spooned over each, or serve
the patties and sauce over hot cooked rice. Makes 6
servings.

Chuck-Wagon Stew

3 pounds beef stew meat
1 can (1 pound) red kid-
  ney beans
2 cans (1 pound each)
  solid-pack tomatoes
1 cup sliced onion
—
2 teaspoons salt
¼ teaspoon ground black
  pepper
1 teaspoon sugar
¼ teaspoon garlic pow-
der or 1 small clove gar-
  lic
3 teaspoons chili powder
—
½ teaspoon dried oregano
  or 2 teaspoons chopped
  fresh oregano
2 tablespoons flour
3 tablespoons water
4 to 5 cups hot cooked
  rice
chopped parsley

Trim the excess fat from the meat and fry out enough
fat from it to brown the meat. Cut the meat into
1-inch pieces, add to the hot fat, and brown on all
sides. Drain the water from the kidney beans and add it
to the meat along with the tomatoes and onion. (Reserve the beans.) Cover and simmer 1½ hours or until

the meat is almost tender. Add the drained kidney beans and the next 5 ingredients. Cover and simmer 30 minutes or until the meat is tender. Add the oregano. Mix the flour with the water to a smooth paste and stir it into the stew. Cook 2 to 3 minutes or until the stew has thickened. Serve hot over hot cooked rice, with chopped parsley sprinkled on top. Makes 8 servings. Serve with a mixed-vegetable salad, corn muffins, mustard pickle, fresh fruit cup and cookies.

CURRIED DISHES

Curried Lamburgers

1½ pounds ground lean lamb
onion salt
6 tablespoons softened butter or margarine

1 to 1¼ teaspoons curry powder
6 hamburger buns, warmed

Shape unseasoned ground lamb into 6 patties ½ inch thick. Sprinkle both sides of each patty with onion salt. Place the lamburgers in a folding wire holder and grill them over slow-burning embers 15 to 20 minutes, turning to brown both sides. Meanwhile, combine the butter or margarine and the curry powder. Spread the mixture generously over both sides of the browned patties. Serve in split, warmed hamburger buns. Makes 6 servings. Serve with potato salad, deviled eggs, sliced tomatoes and cucumbers on lettuce, cantaloupe or honeydew melon and Fruit-and-Nut Cooky Bars.

Indian-Style Lamb Curry

Authentic Indian curry never contains curry powder. Instead, it is prepared with the spices from which curry powder is made. The spices and the onions must be cooked with the fat before the other ingredients are added.

2 pounds boneless leg of lamb

3 tablespoons salad oil, clarified butter, or shortening

1 cup chopped onion

1 clove garlic, chopped, or ½ teaspoon garlic powder

___

1 teaspoon ground cumin seed

1 teaspoon ground cardamon seed

1 teaspoon ground ginger

1 teaspoon ground turmeric

¼ teaspoon ground black pepper

⅟₁₆ to ⅛ teaspoon cayenne

2 tablespoons ground coriander

___

2 cups hot water

1½ teaspoons salt

¼ cup yogurt, or ¼ cup undiluted evaporated milk

1 teaspoon fresh lemon juice

___

3 to 4 cups hot cooked rice

Trim off the excess fat from the lamb. Discard the fat. Cut the lamb into 1-inch pieces and set aside. Heat the oil in a 9- or 10-inch skillet, add the onion and garlic, and cook, stirring frequently, over moderately low heat 10 to 12 minutes or until the onions are very soft and begin to discolor. Add the next 7 ingredients and stir and cook over low heat 2 to 3 minutes, being careful not to scorch the spices. Add the lamb and cook over moderate heat 10 to 15 minutes or until it has lost its pink color. Stir in the hot water and salt. Cover and cook 30 minutes or until the lamb is tender. Remove the cover and cook until the sauce has thickened slightly and has reduced to about half the original amount. Just before serving, add the yogurt or the evaporated milk and heat 1 minute. Stir in the lemon juice. Makes 6 servings. Serve with rice, chutney, yogurt, grapes, diced apples, banana chunks rolled in flaked or shredded coconut, slivered toasted almonds; serve Pumpkin Chiffon Pie for dessert.

DESSERTS

English Apple Pie

If this pie is made the day before it is served it cuts into perfect wedges.

3 pounds tart cooking apples
___
½ cup granulated sugar
½ teaspoon ground nutmeg
¼ teaspoon salt

2 tablespoons lemon juice
___
¾ cup light brown sugar
1 cup sifted all-purpose flour
½ cup (1 stick) butter or margarine

Peel the apples and slice them paper-thin. Mix the next 4 ingredients and blend the mixture with the apples. Pack as firmly as possible in a 10-inch pie plate. Combine the brown sugar and the flour, add the butter or margarine, and cut it in until the mixture resembles coarse crumbs. Sprinkle over the apples and press down firmly, especially at the edges, to help the pie retain the juice. Cover the bottom of the oven with foil to catch any juice that may boil over from the pie plate. Bake in a preheated moderate oven (350° F.) 1¼ hours or until apples are tender. Cool the pie completely, cut into wedges, and serve. Makes one 10-inch pie (8 servings).

Grated-Apple Snow

A delicious dessert that is easily and quickly made.

2 cups grated raw apples
¼ cup fresh lemon juice
⅛ teaspoon ground nutmeg
⅛ teaspoon salt

6 tablespoons sugar
2 large egg whites
grated unsweetened chocolate

Combine the first 4 ingredients with 2 tablespoons of the sugar and chill. Beat the egg whites until they stand in soft stiff peaks, then gradually beat in the remaining 4 tablespoons sugar. Continue beating until the egg whites are very stiff, then fold into the apple mixture.

Serve in sherbet glasses. Sprinkle with grated unsweetened chocolate. Makes 6 servings.

Pumpkin Chiffon Pie

1 envelope unflavored gelatin
$\frac{1}{4}$ cup cold water
$\frac{3}{4}$ cup sugar
$\frac{1}{2}$ teaspoon ground mace
$\frac{1}{2}$ teaspoon ground ginger
$\frac{1}{2}$ teaspoon ground cinnamon
$\frac{1}{2}$ teaspoon salt

1 cup mashed cooked pumpkin
2 large eggs, separated
$\frac{1}{2}$ cup milk
9-inch baked pie crust, cold

$\frac{1}{2}$ cup heavy cream
1 tablespoon sugar

Soften the gelatin in the cold water and set aside. Combine $\frac{1}{2}$ cup of the sugar with the next 4 ingredients in the top part of a double boiler. Blend in the pumpkin and the egg yolks. Stir in the milk. Cook the mixture over hot water (not boiling) until it is thick, stirring frequently. Remove from the heat and blend in the gelatin. Chill over ice water until the mixture mounds when dropped from a spoon. Beat the egg whites until they stand in soft stiff peaks, then gradually beat in the remaining $\frac{1}{4}$ cup sugar. Fold the beaten whites into the mixture. Turn into a cold baked pie crust. Chill until the pie is firm and ready to serve. Put the cream and the 1 tablespoon of sugar in a bowl and beat until the cream stands in soft stiff peaks. Spread the whipped cream over the pie. If desired, sprinkle the top with additional mace. Makes one 9-inch pie (6 servings).

FISH AND SHELLFISH

Crab Cakes

½ teaspoon powdered
   mustard
1 teaspoon water
2 cans (7½ oz. each)
   canned crabmeat
3 egg yolks
2 tablespoons mayonnaise
fine dry breadcrumbs
2 teaspoons lemon juice

dash cayenne
⅛ teaspoon ground mace
   (optional)
salt to taste
flour
1 tablespoon cold water
1 tablespoon butter or
   margarine
2 tablespoons salad oil

Mix the mustard with the 1 teaspoon water and let the mixture stand 5 minutes. Flake the crabmeat and remove the pieces of cartilage. Add the mustard, 2 of the egg yolks, the mayonnaise, 5 teaspoons of breadcrumbs, the lemon juice, cayenne, mace if used, and salt to taste. (Some brands of crab meat do not need salt in addition to that with which they are canned.) Mix the ingredients well. Shape the mixture into 8 cakes. Chill 30 to 40 minutes or until the cakes have become a little firm. Beat the remaining egg yolk with the water. Roll the cakes in flour, dip them into the egg yolk and then roll them in fine dry breadcrumbs. Heat the butter or margarine and the oil in a skillet, add the crab cakes, and brown them quickly on both sides, being careful not to brown them too much. Serve hot. Makes 4 servings of 2 cakes each. Serve with Lyonnaise potatoes, creamed spinach, beet and onion salad with Creamy French Dressing, and English Apple Pie.

Grilled Fish Steaks with Rosemary Butter

For each serving, allow ¼ to ⅓ pound fish steaks (halibut, salmon, or swordfish) cut ½ inch thick. Place the fish over an oiled barbecue grill or in a folding wire holder. Mix 5 teaspoons salt with 1 cup hot water (this is the correct amount of salt) and brush it over the fish at 5-minute intervals or as often as the fish looks dry. Cook the fish approximately 20 minutes over slow-burning embers, turning frequently. Remove from the grill and spread the steaks with Rosemary Butter (see following recipe). Serve promptly. If desired, the fish may be cooked in the oven broiler 15 to 20 minutes. Serve with boiled new potatoes in parsley butter, asparagus, grape and cabbage salad, corn sticks, and Gingerbread with whipped cream or Golden Lemon Sauce.

ROSEMARY BUTTER Blend ½ teaspoon crumbled dried rosemary with ¼ cup (½ stick) softened butter. This butter keeps well if stored in a covered jar in the refrigerator. Makes enough for 6 servings of fish.

Paella

This Paella was developed to be cooked in the oven, to give the hostess more time with her guests. A green salad, garlic French bread, and a dessert complete the menu. Lobster meat may be added to this Paella, if desired.

6 tablespoons olive oil or salad oil

1 pound lean pork, cut into 1-inch pieces

2 pounds chicken breasts and thighs

2 cups long-grained rice

3 cups water

1 pound boneless fish (fillet of haddock or perch fillets)

5 cups hot chicken stock or broth

_____

2 tablespoons salt

1¼ teaspoons dried oregano leaves

1 teaspoon crumbled saffron strands

1½ cups chopped green pepper

1 cup chopped onion

½ small clove garlic, mashed

3 cups diced raw tomatoes, or 2 cups canned tomatoes

_____

1 pound raw shrimp, peeled and deveined

1 cup raw green peas

_____

10 hot cooked artichoke hearts

10 hot steamed clams and/or mussels in their shells (optional)

Heat 4 tablespoons of the oil in a 10- or 12-inch skillet. Add the pork and chicken, a few pieces at a time, and brown on all sides. Soak the rice in the water 30 minutes, drain it well, and cook it in the remaining 2 tablespoons olive oil or salad oil until it is dry and begins to discolor and stick to the bottom of the pan. Turn the rice into a 5-quart casserole or into a 15½- by 10½- by 2¼-inch baking pan or roasting pan. Arrange the browned chicken and pork and the fish over the rice, Rinse the skillet with 1 cup of the chicken stock or broth and pour it over the rice. Mix the remaining 4 cups chicken stock or broth with the next 7 ingredients, and pour over the rice. Cover and cook in a preheated slow oven (325° F.) 40 minutes. Add the shrimp and peas, and cook 20 minutes longer. Garnish the dish with the artichoke hearts and, if desired, with hot steamed clams and/or mussels. Serve promptly. Makes 10 servings.

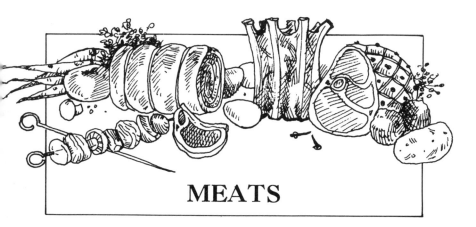

MEATS

Beef

Austrian Goulash

3 pounds boneless beef
    stew meat

---

3 teaspoons salt

¼ teaspoon ground gin-
    ger

1 tablespoon caraway seed

1 tablespoon dill seed

---

2 cups bouillon, or 2
    bouillon cubes and 2
    cups hot water

½ teaspoon ground black
    pepper

---

3 cups onion rings

¼ cup flour

½ cup cold water

---

1 cup sour cream

1 tablespoon Hungarian
    paprika

20-ounce can sauerkraut

Trim off the excess fat from the meat. Discard the fat. Cut the meat into 1-inch pieces and put in a Dutch oven or a 2½-quart baking dish. Add the next 4 ingredients and mix them with the meat. Cover and cook in a preheated slow oven (325° F.) 50 minutes. Add the bouillon or the bouillon cubes and hot water and mix well. Add the black pepper. Cover and cook 40 minutes. Scatter the onion rings over the meat and continue cooking 30 minutes or until the meat and onions are tender. Beat together the flour and cold water until the mixture is smooth, add to the meat, and cook, covered, 6 to 7 minutes or until the sauce has thickened. Stir in the sour cream and paprika, and cook 5 minutes or only until hot—do not let the goulash boil at this point. Heat the sauerkraut in a separate saucepan and serve with the goulash. Makes 8 servings. Serve with tossed green salad, cornbread squares, butter, and pumpkin pie or blueberry pie.

Chili-and-Tarragon Meat Balls

These meat balls are extra-special in flavor. Chili powder and tarragon are an unusual combination, but they blend with and enhance the other ingredients.

1 teaspoon powdered
mustard
2 teaspoons water
_____
1 pound ground chuck
fine dry breadcrumbs
_____
¼ cup finely chopped on-
ion
1 large egg
2 tablespoons soy sauce
⅛ teaspoon ground black
pepper
¼ teaspoon salt
¼ teaspoon instant

minced garlic or garlic
juice
1 teaspoon chili powder
_____
1 tablespoon shortening
1½ cups bouillon, or 2
bouillon cubes and 1½
cups hot water
½ teaspoon dried tarra-
gon leaves or 2 tea-
spoons chopped fresh
tarragon
1½ tablespoons flour
3 tablespoons cold water

Mix the mustard with the 2 teaspoons water and set it aside for the flavor to develop. Put the chuck, ¼ cup fine dry breadcrumbs, the mustard, and the next 7 ingredients in a mixing bowl and mix well. Shape the mixture into 1½-inch balls, roll the balls in fine dry breadcrumbs, and brown them on all sides in the shortening. Add the bouillon or the bouillon cubes and hot water. Cover and cook over moderate heat 15 to 20 minutes. Add the tarragon leaves and cook, covered, 5 minutes. Blend the flour with the 3 tablespoons cold water, add, and cook until the sauce has thickened. Makes 5 servings of 3 meat balls each. Serve with rice or mashed potatoes, snap beans with mushrooms, orange and grapefruit salad, hard rolls, baked apples and cookies.

My Best Liver Loaf

This liver loaf is as delicious cold in sandwiches as it is as a hot entrée.

1 teaspoon powdered mustard
2 teaspoons cold water

1 pound liver (beef, lamb, or pork)
½ cup boiling water

½ pound pork sausage
1 cup soft breadcrumbs
½ cup finely chopped onion

1 tablespoon lemon juice
1 teaspoon salt
¼ teaspoon ground black pepper
1 teaspoon Worcestershire sauce
2 large eggs
½ cup stock from cooking liver

2 strips bacon

Blend the mustard with the cold water and set it aside for 5 minutes to develop the flavor. Slice the liver, place it in a saucepan with the boiling water, and simmer, uncovered, for 5 minutes. Remove the liver from the water, drain it well, and put it through the food chopper, using the medium blade. (Reserve the liver stock.) Mix the chopped liver with the mustard and all the remaining ingredients except the bacon. Turn the mixture into a greased 9- by 5- by 3-inch loaf pan and arrange the bacon strips on top. Bake in a preheated moderate oven (350° F.) 45 to 50 minutes. Makes 8 to 10 servings.

Lamb

Rosemary Lamb Roast

1 medium-sized carrot, sliced
1 rib of celery, sliced
1 medium-sized onion, sliced
6-pound leg of lamb

1 teaspoon crumbled dried rosemary leaves
2 teaspoons salt
½ teaspoon ground black pepper
3 cups water
3 tablespoons flour

Scatter the vegetables over the bottom of the roasting pan. Place the lamb on the vegetables. Combine ½ teaspoon of the rosemary with the salt and black pepper and rub the mixture over the lamb. Pour 1 cup of the water into the pan around the lamb. Roast, uncovered, in a preheated slow oven (325° F.) 2½ to 3 hours or until the lamb is tender. Add additional water to the pan if necessary. Transfer the roast to a warmed platter and keep it warm while making the gravy. Skim off and discard the excess fat from the pan liquid. Add 1¾ cups water and the remaining ½ teaspoon rosemary. Bring the liquid to boiling point and boil 1 minute, then strain, and return the strained liquid to the roasting pan. Blend the flour with the remaining ¼ cup water until the mixture is smooth. Add it to the strained liquid. Bring to boiling point and boil 1 minute or until the gravy is of desired thickness. Season to taste with additional salt and ground black pepper. Makes approximately 12 to 15 servings.

Shish Kebabs

2 pounds boneless lean leg of lamb

---

3 tablespoons salad oil
1½ tablespoons wine vinegar
2 teaspoons prepared mustard
2 teaspoons salt
¾ teaspoon crumbled dried rosemary leaves

¼ teaspoon ground black pepper
1 tablespoon finely chopped onion
¼ teaspoon garlic juice
⅛ teaspoon ground ginger

---

8 squares of green pepper
8 medium-sized mushroom caps
8 tomato wedges

Trim the excess fat from the lamb and cut the meat into
1½-inch squares. Set aside. Combine the next 9 ingredients, add the lamb, and mix well. Cover the bowl and
let the lamb marinate in the refrigerator 5 to 6 hours or
overnight, stirring occasionally to marinate the lamb
uniformly. When ready to cook, string the lamb on
skewers, alternating with squares of green pepper cut
the same size as the pieces of lamb, and with the mushroom caps. Reserve the marinade. Place the skewers over
slow-burning embers on a charcoal grill, or in the oven
broiler, and cook 15 to 20 minutes or until the lamb is
tender, basting with the marinade as often as the meat
looks dry. To prevent overcooking the tomato wedges,
put them on the skewers for only the last 5 minutes of
the cooking period. The cooking time depends upon the
heat of the fire. Serve the kebabs in hot frankfurter rolls
or in other long rolls. Makes 8 servings. At a back-yard
cookout serve the Shish Kebabs in warmed frankfurter
rolls with corn on the cob, carrots baked in foil, and a
green salad or sliced tomatoes.

Pork

Baked Pork Chops with Curry Stuffing

6 center-cut double pork
chops, ½ pound each
salt
ground black pepper
¼ teaspoon ground gin-
ger
2½ cups fine soft bread-
crumbs (about 5 slices
bread)

1 teaspoon curry powder
2 tablespoons finely
chopped onion
1 tablespoon butter or
margarine, melted
1 tablespoon hot water

Ask the butcher to cut a pocket in each pork chop to
hold the stuffing. Combine ½ teaspoon salt, ⅛ teaspoon
ground black pepper, and the ginger. Sprinkle the in-
side of the pockets and the outside of the pork chops
lightly with the mixture. Make the breadcrumbs, using
an electric blender, or by pulling the bread slices into
fine soft crumbs with a fork. Add ¾ teaspoon salt, ⅛
teaspoon ground black pepper, and the curry powder.
Mix well. Stir in the onion, the butter or margarine,

and the water. Spoon the stuffing into the pockets of the pork chops. Close the pockets with small skewers or toothpicks. Place the chops in a baking pan, and bake them in a preheated moderate oven (350° F.) 1¼ hours. Serve hot. Makes 6 servings. Serve with baked apple rings or applesauce, baked sweet potatoes, cabbage and carrot slaw, hard rolls, and fruit jello with custard sauce.

BAKED PORK CHOPS WITH HERBED STUFFING In the preceding recipe, replace the curry powder with ½ teaspoon poultry seasoning.

Spareribs Barbecued Oriental Style

3½ to 4 pounds lean pork spareribs
¼ cup soy sauce
¼ cup dry sherry
¼ cup finely chopped onion
⅛ teaspoon finely chopped garlic
·2 tablespoons brown sugar
2 tablespoons wine vinegar
2 tablespoons lemon juice
3 tablespoons ground coriander
3 teaspoons chili powder
1 teaspoon ginger
1 teaspoon salt
½ teaspoon coarsely ground black pepper

Place the spareribs in a large shallow dish. Combine all the remaining ingredients, heat (do not boil), and pour the marinade over the ribs. Cover and marinate 3 to 4 hours at room temperature. When ready to cook, place the spareribs on a rack in a 15½- by 10- by 1-inch pan (jelly-roll pan). Bake in a preheated moderate oven (350° F.) 1½ hours or until the ribs are tender, turning and brushing with the marinade at 20-minute intervals. If you like your spareribs crisp, place them under the broiler heat 3 to 5 minutes. With scissors, cut the ribs into 2- to 3-rib serving pieces. Makes 6 servings. Serve with baked potatoes, broccoli with Browned Butter Sauce, chef salad with Roquefort cheese dressing, garlic bread, and apple dumplings.

Veal

Rolled Veal-and-Pork-Tenderloin Roast

3½ pounds boned rib roast of veal or boned shank half of leg of veal

1½ pounds pork tenderloin

¼ teaspoon ground ginger

⅛ teaspoon instant
  minced garlic
¼ teaspoon ground black
  pepper
2 teaspoons salt

beef suet
Browned Potatoes (see
  recipe below)
Veal Gravy (see recipe below)

Ask the butcher to roll the pork tenderloin with the
boned veal, having the tenderloin in the center of the
roast, and have him tie it securely. Combine the next 4
ingredients and rub the mixture over the outside of the
roast. Place the roast on a rack in a roasting pan or
baking pan. Insert a meat thermometer in the center of
the thickest part of the roast. Lay pieces of beef suet
over the top to prevent the veal from drying as it cooks.
(If the shank end of a leg of veal is used, cover the
smaller end of the shank with foil to prevent it from
overcooking.) Place the roast in a preheated slow oven
(325° F.) and cook it until the thermometer registers
150° F. Then remove the beef suet (and the foil, if
used) and continue cooking until the thermometer
registers 170° F. The total cooking time is from 2½ to
3 hours. While the meat is browning, baste it 2 or 3
times with the pan drippings. Remove the roast from
the oven and let it stand 15 minutes so it will be easier

to carve. Makes 10 to 12 servings. Serve with Browned Potatoes and Veal Gravy, Carrots Lyonnaise, spiced canned fruit, tray of assorted raw vegetables, hot biscuit, butter, jelly, and Pumpkin Chiffon Pie.

BROWNED POTATOES Allow 1 to 2 potatoes per person. Peel the potatoes and put them in a saucepan with 1 teaspoon salt and 2 inches boiling water. Cover and cook 15 minutes or until the potatoes are about half done. When the meat thermometer in the roast registers 150° F., or about 45 minutes before the roast is done, put the potatoes in the roasting pan around the roast. Roll them in the pan drippings. Continue cooking until the roast is done and the potatoes have browned, turning them in the pan dripping once.

VEAL GRAVY Ask the butcher to give you the veal bones that were removed from the roast. Put them in a saucepan with 1 quart water, 1 teaspoon salt, 1 small bay leaf, 2 beef bouillon cubes, and 3 whole black peppercorns. Cover, bring to boiling point, reduce heat, and simmer 2 hours. Cool the stock and strain. Pour off all but 3 tablespoons fat from the roasting pan and set the pan aside. Blend 3 tablespoons flour with ½ cup of the cold veal stock until the mixture is smooth, then pour it into the roasting pan. Pour in the remaining stock and cook 5 minutes or until the gravy is of medium thickness, stirring to scrape all the browned bits from the bottom of the pan. Adjust salt and ground black pepper. Makes 3 cups gravy.

Hungarian Veal Paprikash

Hungarian paprika may be purchased in foreign food stores, specialty food stores, and in the gourmet department of many department stores.

2 tablespoons shortening
½ cup onion slices
2½ pounds boneless leg of veal or veal stew meat
¼ teaspoon ground ginger
1¼ teaspoons salt or salt to taste
1½ cups veal stock, or

1½ cups water and
1½ beef bouillon cubes
2 tablespoons flour
1½ tablespoons Hungarian paprika
⅛ teaspoon ground black pepper
¾ cup sour cream
3 cups hot cooked rice or noodles

Melt the shortening in a 9- or 10-inch skillet. Add the onion slices and stir and cook them until they are tender, 3 to 4 minutes. Cut the veal into 1-inch pieces, mix with the ginger and salt, and add the meat to the onions. Cook, uncovered, over moderate heat 10 minutes or until the veal has browned, stirring frequently. Add the stock or the water and bouillon cubes, cover, and simmer 1 hour or until the veal is tender. Sprinkle the veal with the flour, paprika, and black pepper. Mix well, and cook over moderate heat, uncovered, 1 to 2 minutes, stirring constantly. Add the sour cream and heat only until the cream is hot (do not boil). Makes 6 servings. Serve over hot cooked rice or noodles, with green peas, braised celery, Orange and Onion Salad, vanilla or pineapple ice cream with crème de menthe, and Butter-Pecan Balls.

POULTRY
AND STUFFINGS

The term poultry includes chicken, turkey, duck and goose. Since all poultry is relatively bland-tasting, almost any herb and many of the spices and seeds can be used to season it. Chicken is the mildest in flavor and is the most popular.

Chicken

Broiled Chicken

2 ready-to-cook broiling chickens, 1½ to 2 pounds each

6 tablespoons butter or margarine
1 teaspoon salt

¼ teaspoon ground black pepper
⅛ teaspoon ground ginger
1/16 teaspoon garlic juice

chopped parsely

Wash the chickens, wipe dry, and split them in half lengthwise. Break the drumstick hip joints and the wing joints so the chickens will lie flat on the broiler pan. Combine all the remaining ingredients except the parsley. Brush the mixture over both sides of the pieces of chicken, and place the pieces in the broiler pan, skinside down. Cook in a preheated hot oven (400° F.) 20 minutes, basting once with the butter mixture. Remove the chicken from the oven, brush both sides with the butter mixture, and place under the broiler 4 inches from the source of heat. Broil 5 minutes, brush with the butter mixture again, turn and cook 5 more minutes or until the skin is crisp and brown. Transfer the chicken to a warmed platter and sprinkle with chopped parsley. Makes 4 servings.

Chicken Legs Parmesan

2 cups soft breadcrumbs
$\frac{1}{4}$ cup finely chopped parsley
2 teaspoons salt
$\frac{1}{2}$ teaspoon dried oregano leaves
$\frac{1}{2}$ teaspoon ground black pepper
$\frac{1}{16}$ teaspoon instant minced garlic, or $\frac{1}{8}$ teaspoon finely chopped fresh garlic

¾ cup grated Parmesan cheese

8 chicken legs (thighs and drumsticks)

⅔ cup (1¼ sticks) butter or margarine, melted

Combine the first 7 ingredients and set aside. Wash the chicken legs and wipe them dry with paper towels. Dip one leg at a time in the melted butter or margarine, then roll it in the crumb mixture, and place it in a baking pan, continuing until all the legs have been buttered and crumbed. Bake in a preheated moderate oven (350° F.) 1 hour or until the chicken has browned. Makes 8 servings.

Cantonese Braised Chicken

1 ready-to-cook chicken, 2½ to 3 pounds

2 tablespoons salad oil

½ cup boiling water

⅓ cup soy sauce

1 teaspoon sugar

½ teaspoon ground ginger or chopped fresh ginger root

1 tablespoon lemon juice

¼ cup sliced green onion

1½ teaspoons cornstarch

½ cup chicken stock or water

3 to 4 cups hot cooked rice

Wash the chicken, cut it into serving-size pieces, and wipe dry with paper towels. Heat the oil in a 10-inch skillet, add the chicken, and brown it on all sides, turning the pieces occasionally and adding additional oil if needed. Combine the next 6 ingredients and pour the mixture over the chicken. Cover and simmer 30 minutes or until the chicken is tender. Transfer the chicken to a warmed platter. Blend the cornstarch with the chicken stock or water, mix with the pan drippings, and stir and cook 1 minute or until the sauce has thickened. Serve the chicken with hot cooked rice and the sauce. If desired, the chicken may be cut off the bones into strips and served with chopsticks, Chinese style. Makes 6 servings. Serve with buttered peas, Chinese cabbage salad with mustard mayonnaise, hard rolls, and strawberries and cream and almond cookies.

Stuffings

When chicken, turkey, duck, or goose is to be stuffed for roasting, make the stuffing and stuff the bird just before it is to be roasted—not earlier, to avoid contamination. Stuffing ingredients may be prepared in advance and refrigerated in separate containers until needed.

Allow 1 cup of stuffing for each pound of ready-to-cook chicken or turkey; ½ to ¾ cup for each pound of ready-to-cook duck or goose.

Orange Stuffing

(*For Duck or Goose*)

6 cups toasted bread cubes (croutons)
½ cup chopped onion
½ cup chopped celery
2 tablespoons chopped parsley
1 ½ teaspoons salt, or salt to taste
1 ½ teaspoons ground thyme
¼ teaspoon ground black pepper
1 ½ teaspoons grated orange rind
1 ½ cups diced oranges
½ cup chicken, goose, or duck stock, or 1 chicken bouillon cube and ½ cup hot water

Combine all ingredients. Stuff the mixture into the neck and body cavities of an 8- to 10- pound ready-to-cook goose; or make half the recipe and spoon it into the neck and body cavities of a 4-pound ready-to-cook duck. An 8- to 10-pound goose makes 8 to 10 servings; a 4-pound duck makes 4 servings.

Sage Stuffing

1 cup (2 sticks) butter or margarine
1 cup chopped onions
½ cup chopped celery
⅓ cup chopped parsley
3 quarts toasted bread cubes (croutons)

3 teaspoons salt
3 teaspoons crumbled or rubbed dried sage leaves
¾ teaspoon ground black pepper
¾ cup chicken or turkey stock or broth

Melt the butter or margarine in a kettle large enough for mixing the stuffing. Add the onions and cook them until they are soft, 5 to 8 minutes. Add the remaining ingredients and mix well. Makes enough stuffing for a 15- to 18-pound turkey.

ALMOND STUFFING   Add 1½ cups toasted slivered almonds to the Sage Stuffing recipe.

OYSTER STUFFING   In the recipe for Sage Stuffing, replace the chicken or turkey stock or broth with ¾ cup oyster liquor and add 1½ cups chopped drained oysters.

SESAME-SEED STUFFING   Add ¾ cup toasted sesame seed to the Sage Stuffing recipe.

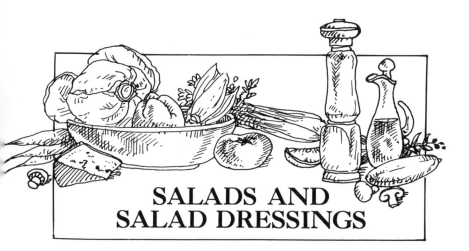

SALADS AND
SALAD DRESSINGS

Salads

The secret of making a good green salad is to use a variety of greens, and have them crackly-crisp, chilled, and dry. Tear the greens into bite-size pieces instead of cutting them with a knife. Then toss the greens with the oil first, being sure that every leaf is coated with oil. This prevents the salad from being watery. Add dried herbs, salt, pepper, and lemon juice just before serving. Toss lightly, to prevent bruising the greens, but mix thoroughly. Avoid adding vinegar or lemon juice too lavishly. If garlic is used, split a clove of fresh garlic and soak in the oil 1 hour; remove the garlic before adding the oil to the greens. If fresh herbs are used instead of dried, add them to the oil along with the garlic, but leave them in the oil to be mixed with the salad. Hearty salads, such as those made of potatoes, other cooked vegetables, or macaroni should be marinated with French dressing several hours or overnight to make them more flavorsome. Do not toss tomatoes with other ingredients, since their juice makes a salad watery; instead arrange them over a tossed salad. Almost all the herbs are natural seasonings for salads.

Orange and Onion Salad

1 clove garlic
¼ cup salad oil or olive oil
2 quarts crisp mixed salad greens—curly endive (chicory), escarole, lettuce, romaine, and watercress
3 medium-sized navel oranges
½ cup white-onion rings
½ teaspoon powdered mustard

1 teaspoon water
½ teaspoon salt
½ teaspoon sugar
1 teaspoon dried tarragon leaves, or 1 tablespoon chopped fresh tarragon (optional)
⅛ teaspoon ground black pepper
2 tablespoons lemon juice or cider vinegar

Split the clove of garlic and soak in the oil for 1 hour. Meanwhile wash the salad greens, dry them well with a clean towel or with paper towels, tear them into bite-size pieces, and put them in a salad bowl. Peel the oranges and cut them into crosswise slices ¼ inch thick. Remove and discard the garlic from the oil. Pour the oil over the greens, and toss until every leaf is coated. Arange the orange rings over the greens, and scatter the onion rings over the orange slices. Soak the mustard in the water 5 minutes and mix it with all the remaining ingredients. Pour the mixture over the salad. Toss gently. Serve promptly. Makes approximately 8 servings.

Spinach and Endive (Chicory) Salad

1 clove garlic
¼ cup olive oil or salad oil
1 small head curly endive (chicory)
¼ pound raw spinach
½ teaspoon salt
⅛ teaspoon ground black pepper
¾ teaspoon dried oregano leaves
1 tablespoon wine vinegar
1 tablespoon fresh lemon juice

Split the clove of garlic, add to the oil and let stand 1 hour. Wash the greens, dry thoroughly with a clean towel or with paper towels, and tear into bite-sized pieces. Place the greens in a salad bowl. Remove and discard the garlic. Pour the oil over the greens and toss until every leaf is coated with the oil. Combine the remaining ingredients, pour over the greens, and toss gently. Serve promptly. Makes 6 servings.

Sesame Seed, Apple, and Celery Salad

3 cups diced unpeeled red apples
2 cups diced celery
toasted sesame seed

3 tablespoons mayonnaise
lettuce or other salad greens

Combine the apples and celery with 2 tablespoons toasted sesame seed and the mayonnaise. Serve on crisp lettuce or any other salad green desired. Sprinkle each serving with ½ teaspoon toasted sesame seed. Serve promptly. Makes 6 servings.

Salad Dressings

Since most cooks have their own pet formulas for French dressing, no recipe is included here. The truly basic French dressing consists of 3 parts olive oil or salad oil to 1 part vinegar or lemon juice, with salt and pepper to taste. Garlic, mustard, paprika, and most herbs, fresh or dried, may be added as and if desired. See the beginning of this section for instructions on mixing salads.

Apple Salad Dressing

½ teaspoon powdered
  mustard
1 teaspoon water
1 large tart apple

3 tablespoons lemon juice
1 teaspoon sugar
1 tablespoon prepared
  horseradish

Mix the mustard with the water and let it stand 5 minutes. Peel the apple and shred it into the lemon juice. Add mustard and the remaining ingredients. Mix well. Serve over fruit salads, salad made of tossed raw vegetables and coarsely shredded cheese, and ham or chicken salad. This dressing will keep 2 to 3 weeks if stored in a tightly covered jar in the refrigerator. Makes 1⅔ cups.

Creamy French Dressing

1 clove garlic
1 cup salad oil or olive oil
½ teaspoon powdered
    mustard
1 teaspoon water
1 teaspoon salt
½ teaspoon sugar
¼ teaspoon ground black
    pepper

1 teaspoon dried basil,
    oregano, tarragon, or
    thyme
2 teaspoons grated onion
⅓ cup wine vinegar
1 small egg white

Split the clove of garlic and soak it in the oil for 1 hour. Mix the mustard with the water and let it stand 5 minutes. Remove and discard the garlic, and put the oil, mustard, and all the remaining ingredients in a bowl. Beat with a rotary beater ½ minute or until the dressing is creamy.

The dried herbs may be replaced by 2 tablespoons chopped fresh herbs. Add the fresh herbs to the oil along with the garlic and leave them in the oil to be mixed with the other ingredients. Makes 1½ cups.

Mustard Dressing

1 teaspoon powdered mus-
    tard
2 teaspoons water
———
2 tablespoons flour
1 tablespoon sugar
1 teaspoon salt
dash cayenne

2 egg yolks
¾ cup water
2 tablespoons salad oil
¼ cup lemon juice or
    cider vinegar
2 egg whites (optional)

Mix the mustard with the 2 teaspoons water and let it
stand 5 minutes for the flavor to develop. In the top of
a 1-quart double boiler, blend the next 4 ingredients.
Beat the egg yolks with the ¾ cup water and the mustard, and add the mixture to the dry ingredients. Stir
and cook over hot water (not boiling) 10 minutes or
until the sauce is very thick. Stir in the lemon juice or
vinegar. If a fluffy dressing is desired and all the dressing is to be used the day it is made, beat the egg whites
until they stand in soft stiff peaks and carefully fold
them into the dressing. Serve over roast beef, ham,
tongue, or cooked cabbage, or use in potato salad, other
cooked vegetable salads, or cole slaw. Makes 1 cup
without the egg whites or 1½ cups with.

SANDWICHES

Asparagus Party Sandwiches

12 cooked asparagus tips,
   3 inches long
3 tablespoons French
   dressing
12 slices firm-textured
   bread
―――
1 package (3 ounces)
   cream cheese

1 teaspoon paprika
¼ teaspoon finely chopped
   onion, or 1/16 teaspoon
   onion powder
1 tablespoon mayonnaise
―――
butter or margarine
12 slivers raw carrot, each
   3 inches long

Drain the asparagus tips well and place them in a shallow flat dish. Sprinkle them with French dressing and let them marinate 2 to 3 hours. Trim crusts from the bread slices, and roll a rolling pin over them to flatten the bread slightly. Combine the next 4 ingredients and mix well. Spread the mixture thinly over one side of each slice. Shape the slices into cornucopias and seal the joining edges with a bit of softened butter or margarine. Place them on a tray, cover with a piece of waxed paper, and then with a damp cloth. Refrigerate until serving time. Just before serving, insert an asparagus tip and a sliver of carrot in the opening of each cornucopia. Makes 12 sandwiches.

Grilled Open-Faced Shrimp Sandwiches

¼ teaspoon powdered mustard

½ teaspoon water

3 hard-cooked eggs

6½-ounce can shrimp, or 1 cup cooked fresh shrimp, diced

¾ teaspoon salt or salt to taste

¼ teaspoon ground black pepper

¹⁄₁₆ teaspoon garlic powder

1 tablespoon fresh lemon juice

3 tablespoons mayonnaise

6 slices firm-textured bread

6 slices tomato, cut ½ inch thick

2 tablespoons butter or margarine, melted

salt and ground black pepper to taste

chopped parsley

Mix the mustard with the water and let it stand 5 minutes. Peel the eggs and chop all the whites and 2 of the yolks, reserving the third yolk. Add the mustard and the next 6 ingredients to the eggs. Mix well and spread the mixture over one side of each slice of bread. Place a slice of tomato on each, brush with melted butter or margarine, and sprinkle with salt and ground black pepper to taste. Arrange the sandwiches on a baking sheet. Place them in a preheated broiler oven, and grill them 5 to 8 minutes or until the tomatoes are done. Put the reserved egg yolk through a sieve and sprinkle a little over each tomato. Garnish with chopped parsley. Serve hot for lunch or supper. Makes 3 servings, 2 sandwiches each.

GRILLED OPEN-FACED CRAB-MEAT SANDWICHES In the preceding recipe replace the shrimp with a 6½-ounce can crab meat or 1 cup cooked crab meat, flaked.

SAUCES

Samples of sauces for appetizers, main dishes, vegetables, and desserts.

Cocktail Sauce

¾ cup catsup
3 tablespoons lemon juice
2 tablespoons finely chopped celery
1 teaspoon finely chopped onion
½ teaspoon salt or salt to taste

½ teaspoon chili powder
¹⁄₁₆ teaspoon garlic powder
1 tablespoon prepared horseradish

Combine all ingredients and chill 3 to 4 hours for flavors to blend. Serve as a sauce for seafood cocktails. Makes 1 cup.

Quick Peperoni Sauce

(*For Spaghetti*)

½ pound ground chuck
½ pound peperoni sausage, cut into small pieces

2½ cups (1 pound 13 ounce can) canned tomatoes
6-ounce can tomato paste
1 cup hot water
½ cup chopped onion
2 teaspoons salt

½ teaspoon sugar
¼ teaspoon instant minced garlic, or 1 clove fresh garlic
1 teaspoon dried oregano leaves
1 teaspoon chili powder
¼ cup chopped parsley
1 can (8 ounces) sliced mushrooms

1 pound spaghetti, cooked
grated Parmesan cheese

Cook the beef and the sausage in a 9-inch skillet 10 minutes or until the beef loses its pink color. Add the next 5 ingredients and simmer, uncovered, 30 minutes. Stir in the next 6 ingredients. Cook 5 minutes. Remove and discard the clove of garlic, if used. Serve over hot spaghetti, cooked according to package directions. Sprinkle with grated Parmesan cheese. Makes 8 to 10 servings.

Butter Sauces

Basic Butter Sauce

¼ cup (½ stick) butter   ⅛ teaspoon ground black
2 teaspoons lemon juice   pepper

Melt the butter in a small saucepan. Add the lemon juice and black pepper. Serve over hot cooked vegetables. Makes ¼ cup, enough for 6 portions of cooked vegetables.

HERBED BUTTER SAUCE   To Basic Butter Sauce, add ½ teaspoon dried herb or 1 tablespoon chopped fresh herb of your choice (basil, chervil, marjoram, rosemary, sage, savory, thyme, or tarragon). If desired, add 1 tablespoon chopped fresh parsley or chopped fresh chives. Serve over cooked vegetables, fish, or shellfish.

Basic Browned Butter Sauce

¼ cup (½ stick) butter   ⅛ teaspoon ground black
                                              pepper

Melt the butter in a small saucepan over moderately low heat. Heat until the butter has browned, 3 to 4 minutes, watching closely to prevent the butter from scorching. Add the black pepper. Serve over hot cooked vegetables. Makes 1/4 cup.

ALMOND BROWNED BUTTER SAUCE Before melting the butter for Basic Browned Butter Sauce, add 1/4 cup slivered untoasted blanched almonds. Heat until the butter is melted and browned. Serve over hot cooked vegetables and fish. Makes 1/2 cup.

PEANUT BROWNED BUTTER SAUCE In the recipe for Almond Browned Butter Sauce, replace the almonds with 1/4 cup chopped peanuts. Serve over hot cooked vegetables. Makes 1/2 cup.

POPPY-SEED BROWNED BUTTER SAUCE In the recipe for Almond Browned Butter Sauce, replace the almonds with 1 teaspoon poppy seed. Serve over cooked vegetables or fish. Makes 1/4 cup.

SESAME-SEED BROWNED BUTTER SAUCE In the recipe for Almond Browned Butter Sauce, replace the almonds with 2 tablespoons sesame seed. Serve over cooked vegetables, broiled fish, or broiled chicken. Makes 1/3 cup.

Dessert Sauces

Foamy Sauce

1 cup sifted confectioners' sugar
½ cup (1 stick) softened butter
dash salt
1 large egg, separated

ground nutmeg
½ cup heavy cream, whipped
½ teaspoon vanilla extract

Gradually blend the confectioners' sugar with the softened butter in the top of a double boiler. Add the salt and the egg yolk. Mix well. Stir and cook over hot water (not boiling) 7 minutes or until the mixture is light and fluffy. Remove from the heat and stir in ¼ teaspoon nutmeg. Beat the egg white until it stands in soft stiff peaks and gently fold it into the sauce. Then fold in the whipped cream and vanilla extract. Serve over puddings and unfrosted cakes. Sprinkle with nutmeg. Makes 2 cups.

FOAMY TIPSY SAUCE   Fold 1 to 2 tablespoons brandy or rum into Foamy Sauce at the time the whipped cream is added. Serve over steamed plum pudding or steamed chocolate pudding. Makes 2 cups.

Golden Lemon Sauce

½ teaspoon salt
1 tablespoon cornstarch
½ cup sugar
¼ cup cold water
¾ cup boiling water
1 large egg yolk
3 tablespoons lemon juice

1 teaspoon grated lemon rind
¼ teaspoon ground nutmeg
2 tablespoons butter or margarine

Blend the salt, cornstarch, and sugar with the cold water. Gradually stir in the boiling water. Stir and cook over medium heat until the mixture is clear and of medium thickness. Mix the egg yolk with the lemon juice and gradually stir into the sauce. Add the remaining ingredients. Stir and cook 1 minute. Serve over steamed puddings, Gingerbread, plain cake, and fruit puddings. Makes 1⅓ cups.

SOUPS

Chili Potato-and-Tomato Soup with Fish Balls

2½ pounds eviscerated whole white fish
6 cups cold water
½ teaspoon ground black pepper
1 bay leaf

1½ cups diced raw potatoes

¾ cup tomato purée
2¼ teaspoons salt
2¼ teaspoons chili powder

18 Fish Balls (see following recipe)

Put the fish, water, black pepper, and bay leaf in a 2½-quart saucepan. Cover and simmer 15 minutes or until the fish flakes when tested with a fork. Transfer the fish to a large cutting board or a large platter. Save the stock. Remove and discard the fish heads, skin, and bones. Use the meat to make the Fish Balls (see following recipe). Add the next 4 ingredients to the stock and bring the mixture to boiling point. Add the Fish Balls. Cover and simmer 20 minutes, or until the potatoes are cooked. Serve hot, in soup plates, with 3 Fish Balls in each portion. Makes 6 servings.

FISH BALLS

meat from 2½ pounds
cooked white fish
1 large egg, well beaten
1 teaspoon salt
1 teaspoon crumbled oregano leaves
¼ teaspoon ground black pepper

Mash the fish, add the remaining ingredients, and mix well. Shape into 1-inch balls. Makes 18 fish balls.

Chilled Tomato Soup

10½-ounce can cream of tomato soup
1¾ cups cold buttermilk
¼ teaspoon dried oregano leaves, or 1 teaspoon chopped fresh oregano
½ teaspoon chili powder
1/16 teaspoon ground black pepper
4 teaspoons sour cream

Combine all the ingredients except the sour cream. Mix well and chill. Serve in bouillon cups surrounded with crushed ice. Garnish each serving with 1 teaspoon sour cream. Makes 3 cups or 4 servings, 1 scant cup each.

HOT TOMATO SOUP   Using the recipe for Chilled Tomato Soup put all the ingredients except the sour cream into a 1-quart saucepan. Mix and heat only until hot. Pour into soup plates, top with sour cream, and serve hot. Makes 3 servings, 1 scant cup each.

Kidney-Bean Chowder

1 pound ground chuck
1 tablespoon butter or margarine
1 cup chopped onion
1 cup diced celery
1 cup chopped green pepper
1 cup beef stock, or 1 cup hot water and 1 beef bouillon cube
2 cans (1 pound each) red kidney beans (not drained)
3½ cups (1 pound 13 ounce can) tomatoes
2 teaspoons salt or salt to taste
¼ teaspoon garlic powder
¼ teaspoon ground black pepper
2 to 3 teaspoons chili powder

Cook the meat in the butter or margarine until it loses its pink color. Add all the remaining ingredients. Cook 20 to 30 minutes, or until the mixture is of chowder consistency. Serve hot. Makes 8 servings.

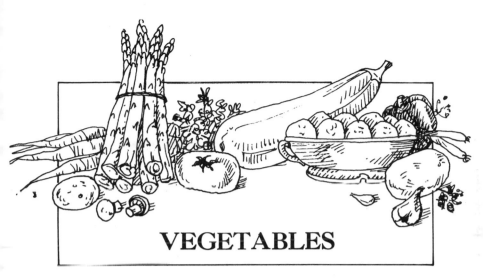

VEGETABLES

Since the range of vegetables is wide, and since all the herbs and some of the spices are especially compatible with vegetables, the seasoning possibilities are almost endless. Examples: basil with new potatoes or peas; curry powder with braised celery, cauliflower, or potatoes; chili powder with zucchini squash or eggplant; oregano with tomatoes, broccoli, or cabbage; nutmeg or mace with snap beans, spinach, or carrots; rosemary with parsnips, turnips, or onions. Or create your own combinations.

Asparagus Baked with Buttered Breadcrumbs

2½ to 3 pounds fresh asparagus

1 teaspoon salt
boiling water

¼ cup (½ stick) butter or margarine, melted

¼ teaspoon ground nutmeg

⅛ teaspoon garlic powder

1/16 teaspoon ground black pepper

2 cups soft breadcrumbs

Break off the tough ends of the asparagus and discard them. Wash the asparagus and remove the scales. In a deep 9- or 10-inch skillet pour boiling water to a depth of 1 inch. Add the asparagus and the salt. Bring to boiling point, uncovered, and boil 5 minutes. Cover and cook only until the asparagus is barely tender, 8 to 10 minutes. Drain off the water and put the asparagus in a 9- or 10-inch pie plate. Combine the remaining ingredients and sprinkle the mixture over the asparagus. Bake in a preheated very hot oven (450° F.) until the crumbs have browned, 5 to 10 minutes. Serve hot. Makes 6 servings.

Carrots Lyonnaise

2 tablespoons butter or margarine

¼ cup finely chopped onion

¼ teaspoon dried thyme leaves

1 teaspoon sugar

¼ teaspoon salt

1/16 teaspoon ground black pepper

3 cups thinly sliced carrots

Melt the butter or margarine in a saucepan. Add the remaining ingredients. Cover and simmer in the butter or margarine only until carrots are tender (about 10 minutes), turning occasionally. Serve hot. Makes 5 servings.

Potato Puffs

1 tablespoon butter or margarine	1 teaspoon salt
½ teaspoon celery seed	2 egg yolks
⅛ teaspoon ground black pepper	¼ cup milk
	2 cups hot mashed potatoes

Add the first 4 ingredients to the potatoes and mix until the butter has melted. Beat the egg yolks with the milk and add to the potatoes. Mix well. Drop potatoes from a tablespoon in mounds onto a buttered cooky sheet, or, if desired, put the potatoes in a pastry bag and pipe in mounds onto a buttered cooky sheet. Bake in a preheated very hot oven (450° F.) 10 minutes or until the potatoes are flecked with brown. Makes 6 servings.

Fried Zucchini Squash and Green Peppers with Tomatoes

1 pound zucchini squash
3 medium-sized green peppers
¼ cup olive oil or salad oil
1 teaspoon salt

1 cup diced tomatoes
¼ teaspoon oregano or oregano to taste
⅛ teaspoon ground black pepper

Wash the squash and green peppers and cut into strips 2 inches long and ½ inch wide. Heat the oil in a heavy 9-inch skillet. Add the squash and pepper strips and fry until they have browned lightly. Add the salt and the tomatoes and simmer 10 to 12 minutes or until the vegetables are soft. Season with the oregano and black pepper. Serve hot. Makes 5 servings.

INDEX